Wild About
BIRDS

Written by Alicia Zadrozny

Reader's Digest

The Reader's Digest Association, Inc.
Pleasantville, New York/Montréal

A Reader's Digest Book

Written by Alicia Zadrozny
Art directed and designed by Karen Viola
Editorial consultant: Kevin McGowan

Illustration and photography credits:
C=Cover, t=top, b=bottom, l=left, r=right, c=center
John Barber: 20b, 21, 23, 24c, 25b
Dan Cole: Cc, 7, 8, 11
Rob Mancini: 9bl
PhotoDisc, Inc.: 4b, 9br
The Reader's Digest Association, Inc./GID: 5r, 6br, 10b, 22l, 24tr, 26-62
Dick Twinney: Ct, 4tl, 5t, 6bl, 10tr, 24tl
Karen Viola: Cb, 5b, 12-19, 20t, 22b, 23b

Address any comments about Build Your Own Birdhouse Book & Kit to:
    The Reader's Digest Association, Inc.
    Adult Trade Publishing
    Reader's Digest Road
    Pleasantville, NY 10570-7000

For more Reader's Digest products and information, visit our website:
www.rd.com (in the United States)
www.readersdigest.ca (in Canada)

Printed in China
1 3 5 7 9 10 8 6 4 2

Contents

Introduction

Right now is a good time to get to know your neighbors—the feathered kind that live high in the trees and fly majestically through the air. There's a lot to learn about these beautiful creatures that sing for us and amaze us with the ability to fly.

Most of us have seen an American robin welcome each spring as it pulls earthworms out of the ground. You may not know that these common birds also enjoy both wild and cultivated fruit.

Most of us have heard the caw of the American crow. But did you know that crows use this sound to warn their kin of lurking danger or to pass on information about new sources of food?

Bird-watching is a hobby enjoyed by people of all ages. Not only is it a fun activity, it also gives us an appreciation of nature, helping us to be respectful of the world around us. Birds add beauty and music to our world, and we can also give back to them. We can do simple things by putting food out for birds and providing shelter for them.

This book and kit is a great introduction to the fascinating world of bird-watching. The fun begins with materials and ideas to build and decorate a home to suit several species of birds.

Clark's Nutcracker

Common Raven

You can further peak your interest by reading about many interesting behaviors of birds, such as their songs and mating patterns. You'll begin to understand how birds seek out different types of shelter and build different nests for their young, according to their species. Then you can try out ways to help take care of birds yourself. This book provides some easy do-it-yourself projects and helpful tips about feeding and providing shelter for birds.

Inside the field guide at the back of this book, you'll learn about 90 bird species common to North America. Use this guide to identify the birds you see. You'll discover the uniqueness of individual species. The notebook makes it easy to record their physical and behavioral characteristics while you're out in "the field." When you're back inside, you can reference the field guide.

You'll come to know a lot more about the world of birds as you distinguish between larks, wrens, and sparrows and listen for the creaking song of the common grackle or the distinctive call of the whip-poor-will. So get going and start bird-watching.

Female

Male

Red-winged Blackbird

Bird Behavior

Birds spend their days just as any other creature does—eating, communicating, sleeping, setting up home, and taking care of family. Birds have many reasons for acting as they do, just like you. What have you seen birds doing?

Learning about the daily activities of birds will help you with your exploration. You can also find more information about the distinguishing behaviors of birds in the field guide at the back of this book.

Bird Song

Surely, you have heard the sounds of birds in your midst. Whether you hear chirping, tweeting, calling, or birdsongs, you are actually listening to a special language used to communicate many things. Members of a flock will call to each other to warn of danger or to tell each other about available food. During mating season, a male bird will sing to attract a partner or mark his territory. A baby bird will cry out to its parents for food.

Members of a hermit thrush flock will use their call to make sure they keep together when migrating. The male song sparrow serenades his mate all day long with as many as 20 different melodies and will vary it nearly 1,000 ways.

Each species of bird has its own unique song, just like how your voice is different from anyone else. With the same yellow breast marked with a black "V" and similar flying patterns, the eastern and western meadowlarks are almost identical—except for their songs. The eastern bird sings with a clear and high-pitched voice, singing lonely, sad songs with three to five notes. The western bird sings a different tune, with five to seven slurred notes and a confident, self-assured performance.

The songs and calls of birds have captivated the most casual bird-watchers to the most dedicated scientists. Ted Parker was one field biologist noted for his work recording birds all around the world. Before his death in 1993, he learned the calls and songs of more then 4,000 species—more than anyone else in history. The sound of the male nightingale wooing his partner has inspired many love poems, including John Keats' "Ode to a Nightingale."

So, when you are watching birds, also make sure to listen to them, too.

Song Sparrow

fun fact
North American Idol
The red-eyed vireo is a noted crooner in the world of birds. The males will perform practically nonstop during the summer months, with the ability to sing more than 20,000 songs in a day to attract their mates.

Groupies: A flock of chickadees forages for food together.

They Flock Together

Most species of birds form communities to accomplish many important tasks. Birds will migrate to warmer climates, raise their young, and find food together.

Northern bobwhites stick together in times of danger. The entire covey—or small flock—roosts in a ring with each member facing outward so they'll stay warm on cold nights. This instinct also provides a clear flight path to escape danger. If a predator gets too close, the entire covey will explode into the air, making a loud whirring sound with their wings.

Black-capped chickadees band together during tough winter months when food is scarce. Flocks of about a dozen birds roost and forage together, flitting from tree to tree while searching for insect eggs. When one chickadee discovers a morsel, the rest of the flock concentrates on the area, too.

If danger lurks, the first chickadee to spot a predator sounds a warning note as the rest of the flock freezes. Then all the birds make noises from every direction. The intruder gets confused from the noises and moves on.

In fact, other species benefit from the community-minded chickadee. Titmice, nuthatches, kinglets, and warblers often travel with them and appear to benefit from this security system.

When raising their young, acorn woodpeckers do it by committee. One pair will lay its eggs, and the members of its extended family pitch in to help incubate them. Then after hatching, all the adult members take turns feeding the younger ones.

As you observe birds, take note of how they interact with their own species and others.

Mating Game

Before eggs are laid in a nest, males and female members of the same species have to get together to start a family. Most birds pick one mate early in the breeding season and they remain together, caring and feeding for the young until they leave the nest. There are some exceptions, though—red-winged blackbirds, for instance, may have multiple mates during each breeding season.

Birds use their songs and other interesting behaviors to woo their mates. Come springtime, you may see some male birds going into full courting mode. Take note of what they are doing and how other birds are responding.

Before they nest, northern cardinals bond at the feeder. The male bird chooses the best seeds and feeds them to the female bird to win her affection. Once this species pairs off, their romance could continue for years. They'll complete each other's songs, and the male will continue to bring his mate morsels of food.

When wooing a potential mate, the lark sparrow acts more like a turkey than a sparrow. To attract a female, he'll strut around with his head held high, wings drooped and dragging, and his tail cocked stiffly over his back. Even after he finds his mate, he is still likely to break into his swagger whenever another "lady" lark sparrow passes by.

Prairie-chickens and sage grouse are among the birds that engage in lek mating. Males of these species gather in large numbers and show off for visiting females. The females choose between the competing males for her mate, but will go off on their own to lay eggs and raise their young.

Dinner Date: The male cardinal brings the female choice morsels to win her affection.

Nesting Instinct

Bird nests take many forms depending on the species, but all are created to provide a safe home for their eggs and the chicks that emerge from them. Birds take several days to make their nests. They will fly back and forth to their branch or birdhouse, carefully selecting the ingredients and incorporating them into their design. Scientists believe that nest building is an instinctive behavior, as birds know what to do without learning from other birds. There are hundreds of kinds of varieties of nests that are made with different designs and materials.

Classic songbird nests, such as that of the scarlet tanager of North America, are bowl-shaped frames made out of twigs, grasses, bark, and lined with mud, moss, and feathers. Often human objects, such as string, animal hair, and even aluminum foil, can be found woven into nests.

Fun Fact

Nest Security System

Some large birds of prey allow smaller birds to build their nest inside their own, much larger, one. This way, the smaller birds may start chirping loudly and warn their larger hosts of impending danger.

During her visits north, the northern oriole will make an intricate pouchlike nest that hangs from the tips of tree branches. If you want to the see the eggs of a brown-headed cowbird, you'd have to find the nest of a vireo or warbler. Cowbirds are known wanderers that do not make time to build nests and instead leave their eggs in the nests of unsuspecting hosts.

You can take this information about bird behaviors out into the field with you. Look around and see where nests are built in your yard and watch for the birds that fly to them.

Scarlet Tanager's nest

Barn Swallows

Birds can be as picky as humans when it comes to choosing a home. Some birds such as woodpeckers, drill holes into dead limbs to make a home for their young. Cardinals, on the other hand, will only build their nests high up in trees. Birds that build their nests in cavities, like woodpeckers, are the type that will nest in man-made birdhouses.

The very social purple martin forms large nesting colonies that return to the same site year after year. These birds will be attracted to apartment-style birdhouses. Phoebes, robins, and song sparrows, for instance, usually build nests on the tops of limbs and might choose to nest in roofless man-made houses, such as roosting boxes and nesting baskets.

When it comes to building your own birdhouse, one size does not fit all. Birds will pick their birdhouse depending on its height off the ground, the amount of space there is to build a nest inside, the

fun fact
Housing Crunch
Most woodpeckers drill a few nest holes into dead wood for convenience and also as insurance from competitive hole nesters. Aggressive house wrens are known to bully woodpeckers out of their newly drilled holes and take up residence instead.

size of the entry hole, and the height of the entrance from the floor. Understandably, a screech-owl the size of a softball will need more living room and a bigger doorway than a teeny house wren.

The birdhouse you will make is designed to welcome several species, including titmouse, nuthatch, and wren varieties. The house should be hung between six and ten feet off the ground. Instead of houses mounted on tree trunks, birds prefer ones that are suspended from

a branch or mounted on a post. This way predators—such as squirrels, opossums, cats, or mice—can't get to them. Also, be sure to locate the house away from busy feeders, where birds would be uncomfortable raising their young.

You can also help out your new friends by setting out nesting materials in your yard. Turn to page 21 for a related project. Whether the bird builds its nest in the house or up in a tree, chances are it will appreciate the wool, string, and rags you leave out.

Happiness for Bluebirds

Of all the birds to build a house for, the bluebird could be the most grateful for your invitation. Three species of bluebirds—the Eastern, Western, and Mountain—can be found throughout North America and have traditionally nested in tree cavities. But bluebirds have lost many natural places to nest in, as more and more land has been cleared with the development of shopping malls, houses, and industrial parks. The birds have also faced fierce competition from European starlings and house sparrows that have taken over their natural homes. Sympathetic humans have taken up their cause and formed "bluebird trails" along roads and paths in bluebird habitats. The North American Bluebird Society has compiled a list of ways to attract and take care of bluebirds at www.nabluebirdsociety.org.

Building Your Birdhouse

Assembling your birdhouse is easy, since the seven wood pieces in your kit are pre-cut and all the holes have been predrilled. All you will need is a Phillips screwdriver and the 20 screws included in your kit.

Refer to the diagram on page 15 for wood-panel labels. You'll notice that there is a drainage hole in the floor, and ventilation spaces near the top of the house. Also, when the "latch" screw is removed, one side can hinge open for easy cleaning.

These are all important features of a properly designed birdhouse.

You can choose to assemble the house first, then decorate it, or decorate the wood panels first, then put them together. Remember, birds prefer a natural, unfinished interior, so make sure only the outside surfaces are decorated.

Step-by-Step Instructions

1. Start with the *floor* piece, *side A*, and 2 screws. Position both screws into the holes, and drive the screws in a little at a time, alternately.

2. Use 3 screws to attach the *front* piece.

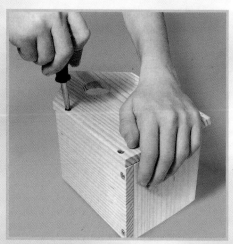

3. Use 3 screws to attach the *back* piece.

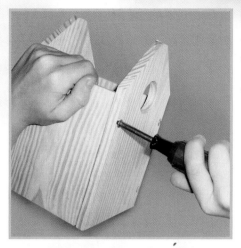

4. *Side B* is the hinging side. Use 2 screws to attach it at the top to the *front* and *back* pieces. Make sure the pre-drilled hole on the edge lines up with the latch hole on the *back* piece.

5. Attach *roof A* to the house. Drive the four screws in a little at a time, alternating between each until the roof piece is firmly attached.

6. Repeat with *roof B*. There are 5 screws for this side. You will have one remaining screw, which will serve as a latch for the hinging side, and can be easily removed when the house needs to be cleaned.

Cutting Pattern

Use this as a guide if you want to make more birdhouses like the one from this kit. Use pine or plywood, ⅜ inches (9 mm) thick.

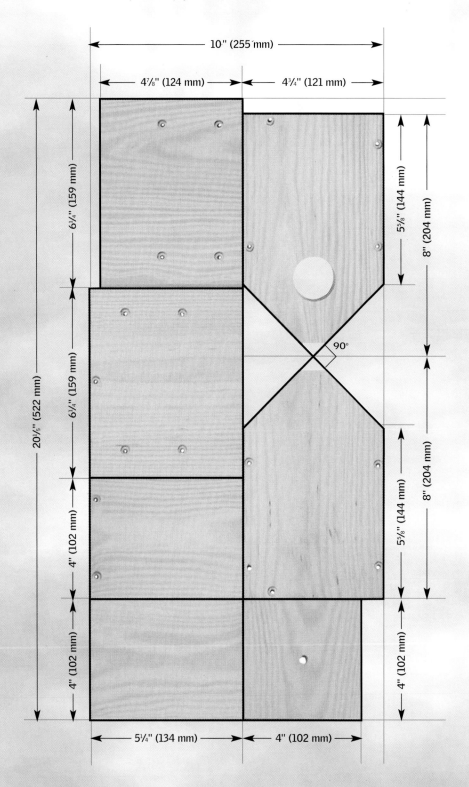

Birdhouse Template

Use this as a guide for hole placement on each piece of wood. Photocopy each piece on this page, enlarging by 400 percent. The black dots indicate the position of each screw. Nails can also be used instead of screws.

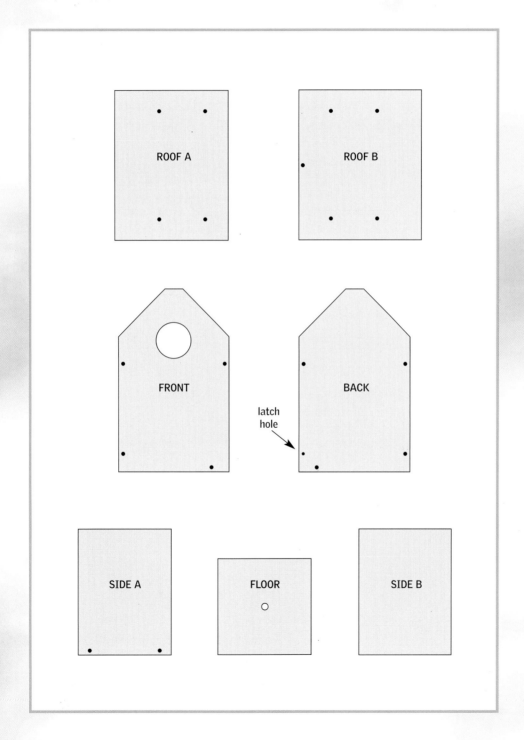

Decorating Your Birdhouse

Have some fun decorating your birdhouse with the included paints and stencils. Birds will be more attracted to a natural-looking home. Plenty of wonderful effects can be created with just a small amount of paint. The more water you add to the paint, the more the natural wood grain will show through—which will appeal to your feathered friends. You can use thicker paint as an accent, along edges, or for stencil shapes.

Use small plastic or paper cups to mix colors and thin them with water. If you make a mistake, the paint will wash off with a damp cloth or paper towel.

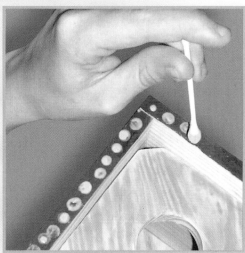

Cotton swabs make it easy to paint circular dot patterns or berries.

17

More Decorating Ideas

Using an all-weather adhesive, consider attaching twigs, stones, sand, shells—or even bits of sea glass—to the outside of the house. Let your imagination go wild!

After your pieces or assembled house is painted and dry, you will need to coat the outside surfaces with polyurethane or another clear finishing spray to preserve your work. If you are spray-coating an assembled house, make sure you stuff the front-door hole with a rag so that the spray won't touch the house interior.

For a fun effect, use wax crayons to draw designs on the wood, then paint over with a wash of color.

Ready for the birds

You can hang your birdhouse in a tree or mount it on a post. Refer to the Housekeeping section on pages 10–11 to keep the birds happy and safe.

If you plan to hang your house, simply feed a length of sturdy wire, cable, or rope through the holes under the peak of the roof and tie or twist the ends together to make a secure hanging loop. Then tie a length of rope to the loop and secure the other end around a strong tree limb.

Put your birdhouse outside in the winter, well before the spring nesting season. If you don't get any tenants at first, your house will be weathered and ready the next season. If birds do choose your house, empty it out by late fall, since most birds will not use a nest a second time. Remove the latch screw and lift the panel. Discard the old nest along with anything else in the house.

Do-it-Yourself Projects

Many people enjoy building and decorating fancy or funky birdhouses. But sometimes the end product is merely a decoration for humans. A rock-and-roll guitar birdhouse may liven up a yard, but chances are many birds may shy from it.

To build a home that is more inviting, people have made birdhouses out of all kinds of natural objects. Birdhouses have been created from dried gourds, hollow logs, or even from vines that have been woven into nesting baskets.

Creating birdhouses is also easy to do with items you have around your own home.

Garden Apartment: Dried gourds make natural-looking homes for cavity-nesting birds.

Home Tweet Home

Many birds nest in holes in banks, ledges, or trees. Here's an easy way to make a birdhouse of your own. Use your binoculars to see what kind of bird moves in.

What You'll Need

- Clean half-gallon milk carton
- Scissors
- Shoe box lid
- Stapler
- 4–6 feet (120–180 cm) of heavy wire
- Wire clippers

What to Do

1. About three-quarters of the way up one side of the carton, cut a round hole about 1-1/2 inches (38 mm) wide. This will be the front of your birdhouse.

2. Use the scissors to punch some little holes in the bottom of the carton. (These will let water drain out in case any rain gets inside.)

3 Punch four small air holes on each side just below where the top folds in.

4. Cut the shoe box lid to make a little roof for the house. It should hang an inch (25 mm) over the edge of the carton on all sides, as in the picture. Staple it to the top of the carton.

5. Poke two holes in opposite sides of the carton about 1 inch (25 mm) below the top fold. Do the same about 2 inches (5 cm) up from the bottom of the carton. Run 2 or 3 feet (50–100 cm) of wire through each pair of holes. (The length of the wire will depend on the size of the post or tree where you plan to attach your birdhouse.)

6. Now attach the birdhouse to a tree or a post that is in the shade, where it won't get too hot. Twist the wire around the tree or post to hold the house in place.

After you build a birdhouse, take it one step further and help birds create their nests. Birds include human objects along with the twigs, leaves, and mud in their nests. Many birds use grasses and other plant parts to build their homes. Why not provide nesting materials in your yard and see if any birds show up to "shop"?

The Best Nest

What You'll Need

- A plastic fruit basket or mesh bag from the grocery store (strawberries are often sold in mesh bags)
- Nesting materials, such as fabric scraps, string, yarn, cellophane "grass," lint from the clothes dryer, hair from hairbrushes or pet brushes, old pillow stuffing, cotton, and thin strips of paper. Use very short pieces of these materials.
- 1–2 feet (30–60cm) of twine or heavy string

What to Do

1. Fill the bag or basket with the nesting materials.
2. Use the string to hang the bag or basket from a branch.
3. Watch birds that visit, noting what they select. Watch the birds as they fly away to see if you can find out where they're nesting.

Feeding Birds

Cedar Waxwing

Bird-watching often begins at backyard feeders and baths. By providing some food and water for birds, you'll get a closer look at them. Birds diets vary—some eat seeds, fruit, and plants; others eat worms and insects.

Supply both kinds of food to see the differences among the birds that dine on them. The diets of individual species are indicated by the size and shape of bird feet and bills. The brown creeper has strong feet for gripping tree bark while probing for insects in crevices with its long, slender bill. The short, strong beak of a finch works like a nutcracker so it can crunch through heavy seeds.

Winter is a great time to feed birds because wild food gets scarce and competition for it increases. The ever-increasing development of land throughout the continent—and destruction of natural habitats—also makes feeding birds even more important. To accommodate your crowd, offer different types of food, like sunflower, thistle, and suet. This way, you'll attract the greatest variety of birds.

Birdbaths, from the most sophisticated marble to a simple basin, will be appreciated by many birds that look for water to drink and bathe in. Finding water sources is also essential for birds during dry summer months.

Birdseed, insect food sources, and feeders to hang from trees or attach to windows are available at your local garden shop and specialty bird stores. Even before you head out to the stores, you can easily provide birds with some of your own foods! Set out grapes, melon rind, and slices of citrus fruits, apples and bananas and watch birds dig in. For another easy bird meal, smear peanut butter on a tree trunk and then poke some peanut bits into it.

Also try to make your own bird feeders and bird treats. It's easy to do and a great benefit for many types of birds.

Milk Carton Feeder

You can make your own bird feeder with a clean and dry plastic milk carton that is a quart or half-gallon (1 or 2 liters).

1. On one side of the carton, cut out a 3-inch (75 mm) square opening about 1 inch (25 mm) from the bottom. Then make a second square on the opposite side.
2. Just below each opening, punch a hole that a straight stick or dowel can fit through. This will be used as a perch.
3. Fill the bottom of the feeder, almost to the level of the openings, with seed, fresh fruit, or mealworms.
4. Tie one end of some string onto the handle of the carton and hang the feeder from a tree or post.

Tweet Treat

Nuts and seeds are rich in fat and protein. They are good foods for birds and other animals because they provide lots of energy. You can make an easy, nutritious snack called "suet" at home.

What You'll Need

Medium-sized pot

Spoon

Beef lard (sold in packages in the meat section of grocery stores)

Birdseed (no exact amount is needed—2 or 3 cups will do)

3-foot-long (1 m) lengths of string

Small plastic containers, such as old yogurt cups

What to Do

1. Ask an adult to melt the lard in the pot on the stove.
2. Let the melted lard cool a bit, then stir in the seeds. If you like, add about 1 pound (½ kg) of oatmeal, raisins, dried fruit, and other tidbits for every ½ pound (¼ kg) of lard.
3. Pour the mix into the containers. Use the handle of a spoon to push one end of the string all the way down through the center of each batch. Tie a knot in the loose end of the string. Let mix cool and harden.
4. Remove the suet from the containers. Turn each one upside down and pull the string through until the knot rests against the suet. With the other end of the string, tie the suet to tree branches.

Tiny Diners

Beautiful, little hummingbirds need to eat almost as much as their body weight in nectar per day. You can provide them a sweet meal with the aid of a special liquid feeder and a simple recipe for sugar water.

Have an adult help you mix one part refined white sugar to four parts boiling water, making sure that the sugar is completely dissolved. Then cover the solution and allow it to cool before filling the feeder.

Create your own feeder with any tiny bottle that has a small mouth. Try using a sterile vanilla or medicine bottle. Tie a bright red ribbon around the mouth of the

bottle and hang it from a branch with colorful pipe cleaners. Fill the bottle with your homemade hummingbird nectar.

Watching Birds

Get ready to spend many hours getting to know the birds around you. In time, you will be able to identify many bird species while learning about their traits and habits. Have fun observing the differences and similarities among species. Don't be surprised if you get quickly hooked, as many bird-watchers do. The most dedicated bird watchers call themselves birders. Maybe you will, too.

Getting started as a bird-watcher is simple—you can set out with what you already have in this kit. Grab that notebook and field guide and you are ready to go. As you practice bird-watching more and more, consider bringing along some binoculars to get a closer look at the birds that sit high in trees. You may even want to bring along a camera and some colored pencils or crayons to record images of birds inside your notebook.

The best time to watch birds is in the mornings or evenings, when they are the most active. Tread carefully and quietly. Sudden movements and loud noises tend to scare off the birds. Remember, when you find your stakeout spot, stay still and make few noises so the birds will not fly away.

You may be able to get birds to fly over to you. Lure them into view by making squeaking sounds or kissing the back of your hand loudly. Repeat these sounds as you watch the birds react.

Serious bird-watchers often use bird blinds—or covered shelters—to observe wildlife. You can practice what these birders do by constructing your own blind with a sheet or bedspread draped over sticks pushed in the ground. Have Mom save the old refrigerator box and cut eyeholes in it for the same effect. Or make it real easy and toss your jacket over your head and zip it up with only your eyes—or binoculars—peeking out.

Look for nests in quieter places in yards—away from feeders, where there is less commotion. Birds often try to disguise their nests so their eggs remain protected. Observe from a distance because birds are very protective of their young.

Your notebook is designed so you can fill in all the important information about the regular visitors to your area. Begin by noting the date, time, and location that you saw the birds. What is the weather like? Most important, what are the birds doing? Are they hopping around? Pulling out worms? What sounds do they make? Note the field marks or spots and stripes of the birds.

When you are out in the field, focus on the birds and record their characteristics. You can always take this information and go back later into the field guide to identify the species. Also, use your notes when you go back to the same spots. See if anything has changed or any patterns become obvious. Try visiting the same places at different times of the day and note any changes.

Over time, you will see patterns emerge among your feathered friends. The same pair of birds that courted and built their nest in the spring might be heading south with the rest of the flock come fall.

I saw the Wren land right on top of the roof!

Date: Saturday, April 19
Time: 10:15 A.M.
Location: Magnolia tree/backyard
Bird Species: House Wren

Observations: Noticed 2 birds (probably the male and female) flitting back and forth between the house and various branches in the tree. They took turns doing this.

Using the Field Guide

Inside this field guide, you can find many common North American birds. Each species is accompanied by vivid illustrations and descriptions of physical characteristics, including size, color, and markings. You will also learn about the natural habitats of the birds, and migration patterns, along with some interesting facts about other traits and behaviors.

Look at the map to discover where to find birds near you during each season and learn about where they are headed next. Many birds breed in northern areas during spring and summer months and then head south for the winter. Other birds remain in one area for the entire year. Next to the maps there are habitat symbols to use as a quick reference.

Remember how birds have that wonderful ability to fly? Well, you just might see a bird that has strayed from its normal range or is visiting out-of-season. As you explore, expect to learn much and encounter surprises along the way. Happy bird-watching!

Bird Parts

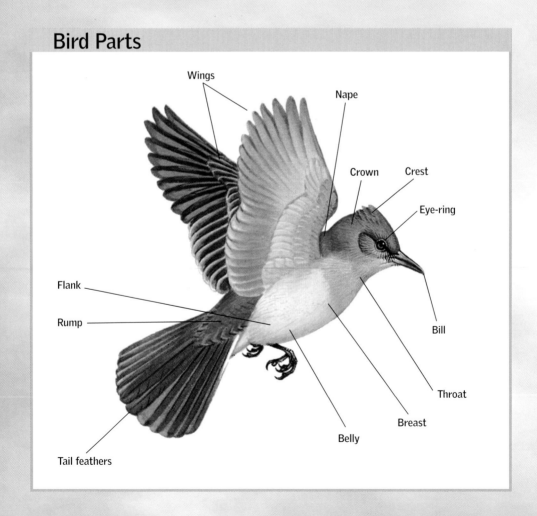

Wings · Nape · Crown · Crest · Eye-ring · Flank · Rump · Bill · Throat · Breast · Belly · Tail feathers

Using Range Maps

These color-coded maps for each species tell when you can expect to see birds in your yard.

Yellow areas of the maps show the summer breeding area. Gray marks the area through which the birds migrate. Blue reveals where the birds winter. In green areas, birds may be found year-round.

Range maps help you identify birds. If you think you see a bird outside of its customary range, it is probably another species of a related family, though sometimes birds stray. When you try to identify a new bird, note the season as you check the range map to find the corresponding color block. This will help narrow the number of species to which it might belong.

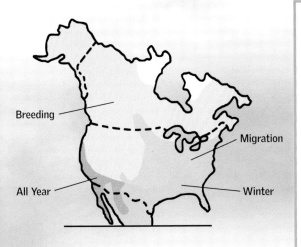

Breeding

Migration

All Year

Winter

 Check marks call your attention to certain features mentioned in the bird descriptions.

Habitat Symbols Key

 Urban/suburban

 Forest

 Grasslands/meadow/beach

 Saltwater

 Freshwater

 Desert

 Compatible with your birdhouse

Pocket Field Guide

Take the Pocket Field Guide included in your kit outside during your bird-watching adventures. It offers descriptions and illustrations of 15 species commonly found in North America. Many of these species are compatible with your birdhouse.

Killdeer *Charadrius vociferus*

LENGTH: 8½"–11" (22–28 cm)

WHAT TO LOOK FOR: two black bars across upper chest; white collar, forehead, spot behind eye; reddish rump and upper tail; wide white wing stripe visible in flight.

HABITAT: prairies, meadows, other open areas, coasts, mudflats, irrigated land.

CHARACTERISTICS: This familiar plover nests on open ground, not necessarily near water. The nest is at best a depression in the ground, but it is defended valiantly when it contains eggs or young. An approaching grazing animal is the object of a threat display: the bird spreads its wings and tail, scolds, and may even fly at the animal. If a potential predator comes very near, however, the killdeer tries to lure it away by playing wounded. With one wing held up over the back and the other flapping on the ground, it waits for the intruder to get close, then runs and repeats the display until the intruder is a safe distance from the nest or young. The killdeer's name echoes its loud, ringing call.

Northern Bobwhite

Colinus virginianus

LENGTH: 8"–10" (20–25 cm)

WHAT TO LOOK FOR: small size; short tail; male reddish brown above, with white on head, black necklace, and streaked sides; female duller.

HABITAT: brushy areas; open pine woods; farms.

CHARACTERISTICS: Both male and female bobwhites help build the nest—sometimes simply a hollow tramped down in a clump of tall grass, but usually with a woven cover of pine needles, grass, and nearby vegetation, with an opening on one side. At night a covey of bobwhites roost on the ground in a circle, with heads outward and bodies touching. This arrangement keeps them warm even when they are covered with snow.

Female

Male

Rock Pigeon (Rock Dove)

Columba livia

LENGTH: 11"–14" (28–36 cm)

WHAT TO LOOK FOR: usually gray, with purplish neck, white rump, and black-banded tail; sometimes white, brown, black, or mixed.

HABITAT: cities, towns, farms.

CHARACTERISTICS: The rock pigeon, originally from Europe and Asia, nests on cliffs in the wild and has easily adapted to the ledges of buildings. Rock pigeons breed several times a year, beginning in March, when the males' ardent cooing is one of the sounds of spring. A mated pair shares the incubation and care of the young, which are fed on regurgitated "pigeon's milk," a secretion from the bird's crop.

Mourning Dove *Zenaida macroura*

LENGTH: 10"–12" (25–30 cm)

WHAT TO LOOK FOR: slim body; pointed, long, tail edged with white; grayish brown above, with scattered black spots.

HABITAT: deserts, brushy areas, woodlands, farmlands, suburbs, parks.

CHARACTERISTICS: The mourning dove's mellow, vaguely melancholy call—*coo-ah, coo, coo, coo*—is repeated again and again, sliding upward on the second syllable and then down for the last three notes. Mourning doves build a flimsy nest of sticks, usually in an evergreen tree close to the trunk. Two eggs make a set. The parents share incubating duties, the male sitting much of the day and his mate during the night. The young are fed by regurgitation, then gradually weaned to insects and the adults' main food, seed.

Yellow-billed Cuckoo *Coccyzus americanus*

LENGTH: 10½"–12½" (27–32 cm)

WHAT TO LOOK FOR: long, slim bird; gray-brown above, white below; underside of tail black, with three pairs of large white spots; yellow lower mandible; reddish-brown wing patches visible in flight.

HABITAT: moist second-growth woodlands; brushy areas near water.

CHARACTERISTICS: Unlike some cuckoos, the yellow-billed does not regularly lay its eggs in other birds' nests—but it is not much of a nest maker, either. The structures of sticks, rootlets, grass, and leaves are shallow and loosely built, and often appear to be too small for a sitting bird and her eggs. From the moment the chicks are hatched almost to the day they fly, they are covered with quills, like miniature porcupines. Then the quills burst open and the feathers bloom out. They utter an occasional *cuk-cuk-cuk*.

Whip-poor-will *Caprimulgus vociferus*

LENGTH: 9"–10" (23–25 cm)

WHAT TO LOOK FOR: mottled brown; rounded wings; white or buff band on throat; white at end of outer tail feathers (male); most active at dusk.

HABITAT: deciduous and mixed woods with clearings.

CHARACTERISTICS: The whip-poor-will calls its name continually and emphatically from a perch in the dark, but its sound seldom gives away its location. The elusive night bird is equally difficult to locate during the day, when it sleeps among the dried leaves of the woodland floor. The female lays two eggs on the ground, without any nest.

Chimney Swift *Chaetura pelagica*

LENGTH: 4"–5" (10–13 cm)

WHAT TO LOOK FOR: small size; dark gray, lighter on throat; bow-shaped wings; short tail; body looks cigar shaped in flight.

HABITAT: open air over woodlands, farmlands, towns, cities.

CHARACTERISTICS: Until humans provided chimneys, wells, and other alternative sites, this dark little bird nested in hollow trees. Chimney swifts pass much of their lives in flight, beating their wings rapidly or holding them stiffly as they sail. They utter a distinctive series of high-pitched chirps. No one knew where chimney swifts wintered until quite recently, when it was discovered that the entire population migrates to a remote part of the upper Amazon.

Western Kingbird

Tyrannus verticalis

LENGTH: 7"–9" (18–23 cm)

WHAT TO LOOK FOR: outer tail feathers white; cap, nape, and back gray; throat white; underparts yellow.

HABITAT: arid open areas with scattered trees or tall brush; wooded stream valleys; farmlands.

CHARACTERISTICS: This species, like other flycatchers, hunts from a perch. It flies out, plucks an insect from the air, and then sails back, often to the same spot. Adults teach their young to hunt by catching insects, disabling them, and releasing them for the young to fetch.

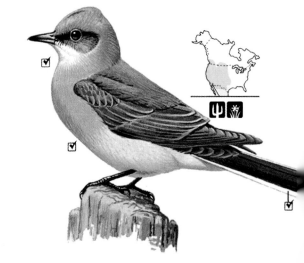

Eastern Kingbird

Tyrannus tyrannus

LENGTH: 7"–9" (18–23 cm)

WHAT TO LOOK FOR: blackish above, white below; dark tail with prominent white band at tip; flies with stiff, shallow wing beats from a high perch.

HABITAT: forest edges; woodlands and open areas with occasional tall trees.

CHARACTERISTICS: Thoreau called this fly-catcher a "lively bird," and wrote that its noisy twittering "stirs and keeps the air brisk." The Eastern kingbird is not only lively; it is fearless in defense of its territory. It will attack any passing crow or hawk, flying at it from above, pecking at the victim and pulling out feathers; it may even land on the flying intruder.

Great Crested Flycatcher

Myiarchus crinitus

LENGTH: 7"–9" (18–23 cm)

WHAT TO LOOK FOR: reddish brown tail and wing patch; yellow belly; whitish wing bars; slight crest.

HABITAT: forests, clusters of trees.

CHARACTERISTICS: This handsome bird announces its presence with a loud, clear *wheep* or rolling *crrreep*. The great crested flycatcher always nests in a cavity—an abandoned woodpecker hole, a hollow tree, or a nest box. If the hole is too deep, the birds will fill it up from the bottom with debris before beginning the nest of twigs. They may add a cast-off snakeskin or a strip of shiny plastic, which is sometimes left hanging outside the cavity.

Say's Phoebe *Sayornis saya*

LENGTH: 6"–7½" (15–19 cm)

WHAT TO LOOK FOR: lower breast and belly rusty; upper parts grayish; tail blackish; wags tail.

HABITAT: open desert, semi-arid areas, ranchlands, brushy fields, canyon mouths.

CHARACTERISTICS: This dry-country flycatcher replaces the eastern phoebe in much of the West and has similar habits. It is a tail wagger, and it often nests on or around ranch buildings. Its call, however, is different—a low, plaintive *phee-eur*. Its customary perch is on top of a small bush, a tall weed stalk, or a low rock. In the northern portion of its range, say's phoebe is migratory, but it is a year-round resident in warmer areas.

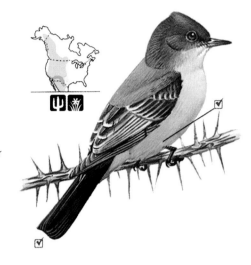

Eastern Phoebe *Sayornis phoebe*

LENGTH: 5"–7" (13–17 cm)

WHAT TO LOOK FOR: brownish olive above, with darker head; whitish below, with gray breast; sits upright on perch and wags tail frequently.

HABITAT: woodlands, farmlands, suburbs; usually near water.

CHARACTERISTICS: *Fibrit,* says the eastern phoebe emphatically from its perch, wagging its tail in characteristic motion. Phoebes are not shy. Often they are found in or on porches, garages, barns, and bridges, nesting on a ledge or beam. This species made ornithological history in 1803 when Audubon tied silver thread on the legs of nestlings—the first North American experiment in bird banding. The next year he found that two of his marked birds had returned and were nesting nearby.

Western Flycatcher

Empidonax difficilis/Empidonax occidentalis

LENGTH: 5"–6" (13–15 cm)

WHAT TO LOOK FOR: yellow throat and belly; olive-brown back; whitish eye ring and wing bars.

HABITAT: moist coniferous and mixed forests, deciduous groves, wooded canyons.

CHARACTERISTICS: The western flycatcher is actually two species separated by geography, the Pacific-slope (*Empidonax difficilis*) of the coast and the cordilleran (*Empidonax occidentalis*) of the Rockies. The green moss nest of the Western flycatcher, lined with shredded bark, is always located in damp wood—often near a stream or under the lip of a streambank. It may also build as high as 30 feet (9.2 m) up in a tree.

Least Flycatcher *Empidonax minimus*

LENGTH: 4½"–5" (11–13 cm)

WHAT TO LOOK FOR: small size; belly white or pale yellow; head and back olive-gray; whitish eye ring and wing bars.

HABITAT: open forests, orchards, rural towns, suburbs, parks.

CHARACTERISTICS: The least flycatcher is noisy during the breeding season. Its curt *chebec* is given as often as 75 times a minute, and it may go on repeating itself for several hours at a time. The male sometimes adds a warble—*chebec-trree-treo, chebec-treee-chou*. Other notes include one-syllable *whit* calls. The species nests in both conifers and deciduous trees, usually quite low but at times as high as 60 feet (18 m). The deep little cup is frequently nestled in the crotch of a limb; materials include shreds of bark, plant down, spiderweb, fine woody stems, and grasses. Southerly nesters may raise two broods a year.

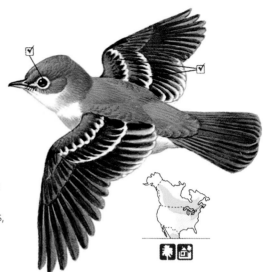

Olive-Sided Flycatcher

Contopus borealis

LENGTH: 6"–71/2" (15–19 cm)

what to look for: grayish brown above, white below, with brown vest; white patch below wing sometimes visible.

HABITAT: coniferous and mixed woodlands, forest-edged bogs, swamps with dead trees; eucalyptus groves (California).

CHARACTERISTICS: Perched on top of a tall tree or dead snag, the olive-sided flycatcher whistles a cheery pip-whee-beer. The first note, pip, is inaudible at a distance, but the rest of the song is high and clear. When alarmed, this husky flycatcher calls pip-pip-pip.

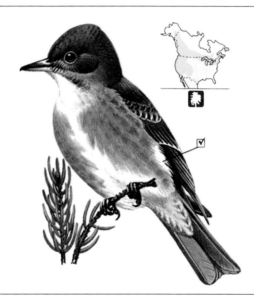

American Pipit *Anthus rubescens*

LENGTH: 5"–6½" (13–17 cm)

WHAT TO LOOK FOR: slim shape; thin bill; dark above, streaked below (breeding bird paler, less streaked); white outer tail feathers; frequently wags tail.

HABITAT: tundra, alpine meadows; grasslands, beaches, coasts (migration).

CHARACTERISTICS: This is the most widespread of the pipits. This species walks, instead of hopping like the sparrows they resemble. (Pipits and sparrows actually belong to two very different families.) In courtship, singing males fly almost straight up as high as 200 feet (61.5 m), then float down on fluttering wings.

Steller's Jay *Cyanocitta stelleri*

LENGTH: 11½"–13½" (29–34 cm)

WHAT TO LOOK FOR: crest long, sharp-pointed, blackish; face streaked with white; upper back and breast blackish; dark blue wings and tail.

HABITAT: pine-oak and coniferous forests.

CHARACTERISTICS: A characteristic habit of jays is the way they land on a tree near the bottom and then work upward, hopping from branch to branch until they reach the top. Then they leave, perhaps to repeat the maneuver. Steller's jays, build bulky nests of dead leaves and twigs, usually near the trunk of a conifer.

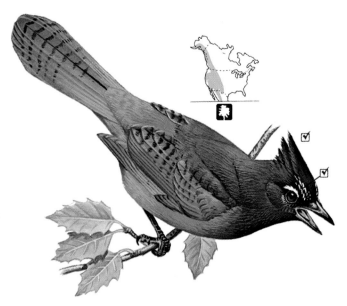

Blue Jay *Cyanocitta cristata*

LENGTH: 9½"–12" (24–30 cm)

WHAT TO LOOK FOR: pointed crest; black necklace; bright blue above, with white on wings and tail.

HABITAT: woodlands, farmlands, suburbs, city parks.

CHARACTERISTICS: This handsome, noisy bird is known for its raucous voice and the wide variety of its calls, cries, and screams. But like other jays, it also has a "whisper song," a series of faint whistles and soft, sweet notes delivered from a perch hidden in foliage. Blue jays are omnivorous, feeding on (among other things) fruits, seed, nuts, insects, birds' eggs, small birds, mice, tree frogs, snails, and even fish. In spring and fall these jays migrate in flocks that sometimes number in the hundreds.

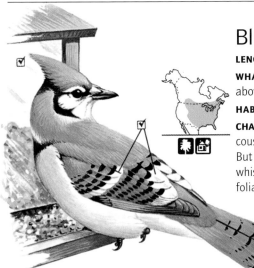

Clark's Nutcracker

Nucifraga columbiana

LENGTH: 12"–13" (30–33 cm)

WHAT TO LOOK FOR: body light gray; wings and tail black, with white patches; bill long, pointed.

HABITAT: coniferous forests near tree line; lower slopes, isolated groves.

CHARACTERISTICS: William Clark, of the Lewis and Clark expedition, thought this bird was a woodpecker, but the leading American ornithologist of the day, Alexander Wilson, called it a crow. Clark's nutcracker has the woodpecker's bounding flight at times; at other times it flies more directly, like a crow. It hammers at cones and nuts like a woodpecker, and robs the nests of other birds, as crows do.

Black-billed Magpie
Pica pica

LENGTH: 17½"–21½" (44–55 cm)

WHAT TO LOOK FOR: tail long, tapering, metallic green; bold black-and-white pattern in flight.

HABITAT: open forests; brushy areas of prairies and foothills; bottomland groves; ranches.

CHARACTERISTICS: This conspicuous, long-tailed species constructs a particularly strong nest in a bush or low in a tree. Sticks, often thorny, make up the base and walls. Mud or fresh dung mixed with vegetation is packed inside, and the cup is lined with roots, stems, and hair. Over the nest the birds build a dome of sticks—again, often thorny.

American Crow *Corvus brachyrhynchos*

LENGTH: 16"–20" (41–50 cm)

WHAT TO LOOK FOR: glossy black, with black bill, legs, and feet; rounded wings and square tail.

HABITAT: forests; woods near water; open areas; farmlands; suburbs.

CHARACTERISTICS: Judged by human standards, crows are perhaps the most intelligent of birds. They can count at least to three or four; they quickly learn new information; they appear to have a complex language and well-developed social structure. North America has three kinds, the American crow and two smaller species usually found near the shore—the Northwestern (*Corvus caurinus*) and the fish crow (*Corvus ossifragus*). A Mexican species also visits Texas. Common and Chihuahuan ravens (*Corvus corax* and *Corvus cryptoleucus*), are often mistaken for crows.

Tree Swallow

Tachycineta bicolor

LENGTH: 4½"–5½" (11–14 cm)

WHAT TO LOOK FOR: glossy blue-black or greenish above (immature dark brown), white below; tail slightly forked.

HABITAT: open areas with scattered trees and dead stubs; usually near water.

CHARACTERISTICS: This is the hardiest swallow, arriving early in spring and even wintering over in some localities. When insects are unavailable, tree swallows feed mostly on bayberries; some wintering birds have also been seen picking seed from pond ice. Tree swallows will nest in birdhouses and mailboxes, as well as in holes in dead tree stubs, their natural nesting sites. In fall the brown-backed immatures can be mistaken for bank swallows (*Riparia riparia*), which have brown "collars," and for northern rough-winged swallows (*Stelgidopteryx serripennis*), which have a brown wash on the throat. In the West, adult birds can be confused with violet-green swallows (*Tachycineta thalassina*), a species with more white on the lower back.

Cliff Swallow

Petrochelidon pyrrhonota

LENGTH: 5"–6" (13–15 cm)

WHAT TO LOOK FOR: mostly dark above; light forehead; rusty rump and throat; square tail.

HABITAT: open country cliffs, farmlands with bridges or buildings for nesting; usually near water.

CHARACTERISTICS: After it was reported from Hudson Bay in 1772, no naturalist mentioned the cliff swallow until 1815, when Audubon found a few in Kentucky. From then on, the birds were seen in many parts of North America. Cliff swallow population began growing as they gradually discovered suitable nest sites under the eaves of houses and barns (cliffsides are their natural nest sites). These are the swallows that return to the Mission of San Juan Capistrano, in California, on or about March 19 each year.

Barn Swallow

Hirundo rustica

LENGTH: 5½"–7" (14–18 cm)

WHAT TO LOOK FOR: tail deeply forked; glossy dark blue above; light rufous below, with darker throat.

HABITAT: open woodlands, other open areas, farmlands, suburbs.

CHARACTERISTICS: Like the cliff swallow, this species has benefited from man's constructions, building its mud nest in culverts, under wharves and bridges, and inside sheds, garages, and barns. The barn swallow feeds almost entirely on insects, which it picks out of the air in its swift, graceful flight; often it will dart close to the surface of a pond, splashing itself from time to time. Before the start of the fall migration, barn swallows join with other swallow species to form huge flocks that rest and preen on telephone wires.

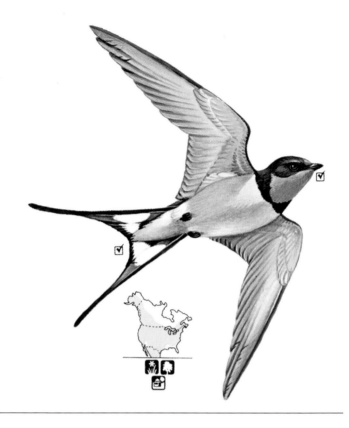

Purple Martin

Progne subis

LENGTH: 7"–8" (18–20 cm)

WHAT TO LOOK FOR: largest swallow; tail slightly forked; male glossy blue-black; female duller above, with mottled throat and whitish belly.

HABITAT: open areas, scattered woodlands, farmlands, suburbs; usually near water.

CHARACTERISTICS: Purple martins have a long history of nesting in shelters supplied by man. In the past they used hollow gourds hung by Indians, and today the species is largely dependent on martin houses. These birds have a strong homing instinct, demonstrated by a colony that returned one spring to find its apartment house gone. The martins hovered and circled at the precise spot in midair where the house had been.

Female

Male

Black-capped Chickadee

Poecile atricapilla

LENGTH: 4½"–5½" (11–14 cm)

WHAT TO LOOK FOR: mostly light gray; black cap and throat; white cheek patch.

HABITAT: mixed and deciduous forests, suburbs, parks.

CHARACTERISTICS: Chickadees that look somewhat alike can often be told apart by their sounds. *Fee-bee*, the black-capped chickadee whistles, the first note of the song a full tone higher than the second. Its call is the familiar *chick-a-dee.*

Tufted Titmouse

Parus bicolor

LENGTH: 5½"–6" (14–15 cm)

WHAT TO LOOK FOR: gray with buff flanks; gray crest.

HABITAT: deciduous forests, cypress swamps, pine woods, wooded bottomlands, orchards, suburbs.

CHARACTERISTICS: Long regarded as a southern species, the tufted titmouse has been spreading northward in recent years. Now these tame, trusting birds are familiar visitors at feeders from Michigan to New England. Their ringing song varies; usually it is a rapid two-note whistle—*pe-ter, pe-ter.* Titmice are relatives of the chickadees, and this species has a number of chickadee-like calls.

White-breasted Nuthatch

Sitta carolinensis

LENGTH: 5"–6" (13–15 cm)

WHAT TO LOOK FOR: black crown and nape; blue-gray above, white below; bill long, straight.

HABITAT: mixed and deciduous forests, woods; groves; suburbs.

CHARACTERISTICS: The nuthatches are the only birds that habitually climb down tree trunks headfirst, gathering insects and insect eggs from crevices and under the bark. The name nuthatch derives from *nut-hack,* for the way the birds wedge nuts and other food into crevices and chop them into pieces.

Red-breasted Nuthatch

Sitta canadensis

LENGTH: 3½"–4½" (89–114 mm)

WHAT TO LOOK FOR: white line above eye; black cap; blue-gray back; reddish underparts.

HABITAT: coniferous forests; mixed woodlands (in winter).

CHARACTERISTICS: The red-breasted nuthatch usually digs its nest hole in dead wood, but it may also use natural cavities, old woodpecker holes, and nest boxes. Whatever site it chooses, it always smears the entrance hole with pitch from spruce, fir, or pine, perhaps to discourage predators. This nuthatch is an active little bird, scurrying over tree trunks and branches, dashing from tree to tree, and calling *yna, yna, yna, yna* in a thin, nasal voice. The white-breasted species has a lower-pitched call.

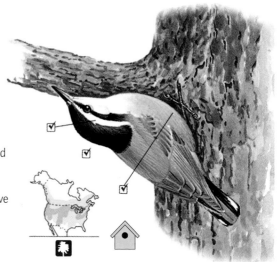

Brown Creeper *Certhia americana*

LENGTH: 4½"–5½" (11–14 cm)

WHAT TO LOOK FOR: streaked brown above, white below; bill long, slender, curved down.

HABITAT: mixed and coniferous forests, groves, woods.

CHARACTERISTICS: The spring song of the brown creeper is a high, sweet phrase, surprisingly different from its usual thin *sssst*. But since the spring song is ventriloquistic, the bird can be difficult to locate. In feeding, the brown creeper invariably flies to the bottom of a tree and gradually hitches its way up the trunk in its search for insects. Then it drops to the bottom of another tree and begins hitching upward once again.

House Wren *Troglodytes aedon*

LENGTH: 4"–5" (10–13 cm)

WHAT TO LOOK FOR: gray-brown above, lighter below, with barring on wings and tail; tail often held erect.

HABITAT: open woodlands, forest edges, shrubby areas, suburbs, parks.

CHARACTERISTICS: House wrens are aggressive and adaptable nesters. They will build their nests in just about any container left out in the open—flowerpot, empty tin can, pocket of an old coat—as well as tree holes and nest boxes. They often bully other birds, ejecting them from nest sites and even destroying eggs and young. Two broods a season are raised. The male frequently changes partners in mid-season, so that while his original mate is still feeding chicks, another female is sitting on new eggs.

Carolina Wren *Thryothorus ludovicianus*

LENGTH: 4½"–5½" (11–14 cm)

WHAT TO LOOK FOR: wide white eye stripe; rufous above, with white throat and tawny sides.

HABITAT: forests with dense undergrowth; scrubby areas; thickets; brush near water; suburbs.

CHARACTERISTICS: The loud, ringing call of the Carolina wren is one of the most common sounds of the southeastern woods, where it is heard even in winter. The call is usually a series of double or triple notes, written as *cheery, cheery, cheery* or *tea-kettle, tea-kettle, tea-kettle*. The bird has been called "mocking wren" because it sometimes sounds like a catbird, a kingfisher, or certain other kinds of birds.

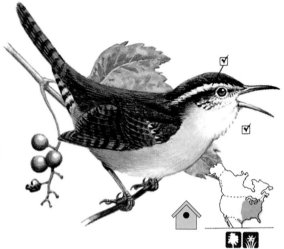

Winter Wren *Troglodytes troglodytes*

LENGTH: 3"–4" (75–102 mm)

WHAT TO LOOK FOR: small size; reddish brown, with dark barring on flanks; very short tail.

HABITAT: coniferous and mixed forests with heavy undergrowth, often near streams; wooded swamps.

CHARACTERISTICS: The song of the winter wren is clear, rapid, and very high in pitch, often with notes beyond the range of human ears. The wren sings along at 16 notes a second, stringing beautiful, tinkling passages into long pieces. It sings over the sound of surf on remote Alaskan islands, where it nests on cliffs and rocky slopes near the shore. Elsewhere it is most often a bird of the deep woods, nesting in the earth that clings to the roots of fallen trees, under standing roots, or in crevices between rocks.

Bewick's Wren *Thryomanes bewickii*

LENGTH: 4½"–5½" (11–14 cm)

WHAT TO LOOK FOR: white eye stripe; brown above, white below; tail long, with white spots on outer feathers.

HABITAT: woodlands, brushy areas, chaparral, suburbs.

CHARACTERISTICS: Audubon named this species for a British friend, Thomas Bewick (pronounced "buick"), whose wood engravings of birds were famous in his day. Though somewhat larger than the house wren, Bewick's wren is less aggressive, and it usually loses out when the two species compete for space. Its diet, like that of all wrens, consists almost entirely of insects, spiders, and other small invertebrates; Bewick's wren in particular is credited with destroying many injurious species such as scale insects and bark beetles.

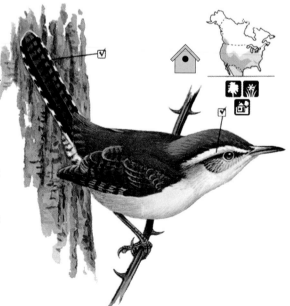

Northern Mockingbird

Mimus polyglottos

LENGTH: 9"–11" (23–28 cm)

WHAT TO LOOK FOR: gray above, whitish below; tail long, blackish; white wing patches; white outer tail feathers; no black eye mask.

HABITAT: open areas, farmland, suburbs, parks; scrubby growth near water (dry areas).

CHARACTERISTICS: Within its range the mockingbird is much more common than the similarly colored shrikes. It is best known for its song, which may be heard day or night. Typically the bird repeats a phrase over and over (perhaps half a dozen times), then drops that phrase and goes on to another. Often the phrases are imitations of other birds' songs, and "mockers" have also been known to sound like frogs, crickets, and dogs, among others. They do not need a recent reminder, it seems, but can remember phrases for several months at least.

Loggerhead Shrike

Lanius ludovicianus

LENGTH: 7"–9½" (18–24 cm)

WHAT TO LOOK FOR: gray above, with black mask; paler below; bill short, heavy; wings black, with white patches; outer tail feathers white.

HABITAT: open areas with scattered trees and shrubs.

CHARACTERISTICS: Both the loggerhead shrike and the rarer Northern shrike (*Lanius excubitor*) are nicknamed "butcher-birds." They kill insects, snakes, rodents, and small birds, then impale them on thorns or barbed wire or jam them into twig forks. Often they build up sizable larders. Evidently, however, the purpose of this habit is more than storage against lean times. For although the shrikes have hooked, hawklike bills, they lack powerful, hawklike feet and apparently must fix the prey on something firm before tearing it with the bill.

Gray Catbird

Dumetella carolinensis

LENGTH: 7"–9" (18–23 cm)

WHAT TO LOOK FOR: long tail; dark gray, with black cap and rusty undertail.

HABITAT: undergrowth in woodlands, hedgerows, brushy areas, suburbs, parks.

CHARACTERISTICS: Often in the nesting season this trim bird is a close neighbor of man. Like the mockingbird, the gray catbird is regarded as a mimic, but it is less an actual imitator than a plagiarist of musical ideas. As one listener put it, the catbird "suggests the songs of various birds—never delivers the notes in their way!" It burbles along, now loud, now soft, uttering a long run of squeaky phrases, seldom repeating itself. It gets its name from its call note—a petulant, catlike mew.

Brown Thrasher

Toxostoma rufum

LENGTH: 9½"–11" (24–28 cm)

WHAT TO LOOK FOR: long tail; bright reddish brown above; two white wing bars; white below, streaked with brown.

HABITAT: open brushy areas, forest edges, hedgerows, thickets, suburbs, parks.

CHARACTERISTICS: Thrashers, like mockingbirds and catbirds, are members of the mimic thrushes family. (The name thrasher derives from the word *thrush*.) A characteristic of this group is the imitation of sounds. The most notable quality of the thrasher's music, aside from the occasional imitation, is the phrasing. The loud, ringing song has been written in this vein: "*Hurry up, hurry up; plow it, plow it; harrow it; chuck; sow it, sow it, sow it; chuck-chuck, chuck-chuck; hoe it, hoe it.*" The bird is usually seen singing from a high perch out in the open.

American Robin

Turdus migratorius

LENGTH: 9"–11" (23–28 cm)

WHAT TO LOOK FOR: bright reddish orange below; dark gray above (head paler on female), with broken eye ring and white-tipped tail; immature with light, speckled breast.

HABITAT: open forests, farmlands, suburbs, parks; sheltered areas with fruit on trees (winter).

CHARACTERISTICS: The robin, a member of the thrush family, is one of the most neighborly of birds. A pair will often build their nest—a neat cup of mud and grasses—on a branch of a dooryard tree or on the ledge of a porch; and they hunt confidently for earthworms on the lawn and in the garden, regardless of human activities nearby. Robins eat insects as well as worms; they also like fruit, both wild and cultivated.

Immature

Wood Thrush

Hylocichla mustelina

LENGTH: 7½"–8½" (19–22 cm)

WHAT TO LOOK FOR: head and upper back reddish brown; white below, with large, dark brown spots from throat to belly.

HABITAT: moist deciduous forests, suburbs, parks.

CHARACTERISTICS: This thrush nests in dark, damp woods, where it builds a tidy cup of grasses, stems, and dead leaves, usually mixed with mud and lined with roots. Often strips of birch bark, paper, or white cloth are woven into the structure. The wood thrush's song is complex and beautiful—a series of brief, liquid phrases often interspersed with a high trill.

Mountain Bluebird

Sialia currucoides

LENGTH: 6"–7½" (15–19 cm)

WHAT TO LOOK FOR: male sky blue above, light blue below; female mostly gray, with some blue; immature grayer, with streaked underparts.

HABITAT: open high-elevation areas with scattered trees and brush; sometimes in lowlands.

CHARACTERISTICS: Both the Eastern and the Western bluebird (*Sialia mexicana*) hunt for insects by scanning the ground from perches on wires or fence posts and then dropping on the prey. The mountain bluebird, which eats a greater proportion of insects than the other two do (seed and berries are also part of the diet), does more of its hunting in the air. It darts out from a perch to catch a flying insect, or flies over the ground and hovers, then pounces. Like other bluebirds, this one nests in cavities, especially old woodpecker diggings; it also uses birdhouses and holes in cliffs and banks.

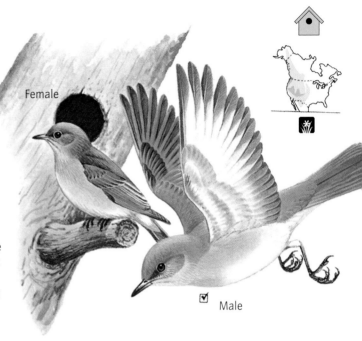

Female

Male

Female

Male

Eastern Bluebird

Sialia sialis

LENGTH: 5"–7" (13–18 cm)

WHAT TO LOOK FOR: male bright blue above, with orange-red throat and breast; female paler; immature mostly gray, spotted with white on back and breast.

HABITAT: open areas with scattered trees and fencerows; farmlands, orchards, suburbs.

CHARACTERISTICS: The sweet *chirrup* and the flash of blue in garden or orchard or along a rural road have made the Eastern bluebird a special favorite. But for many years this much-admired bird has been in trouble; introduced house sparrows and starlings have taken over its preferred tree holes. Fortunately, bluebirds will nest in birdhouses specially designed to keep out the alien intruders. In many areas, hundreds of these houses have been set up along "bluebird trails"— ambitious projects that have halted the species' decline and even reversed it in some places.

Cedar Waxwing

Bombycilla cedrorum

LENGTH: 5 1/2"–7 1/2" (14–19 cm)

what to look for: crest; mostly soft brown, with black face pattern, yellow-tipped tail, and red spots on wing; immature with brown streaks.

HABITAT: open forests, areas with scattered trees, wooded swamps, orchards, suburbs.

CHARACTERISTICS: Cedar waxwings are a particularly sociable species. Pairs of this species have been seen passing berries back and forth. The birds wander in flocks whose arrivals and departures are unpredictable.

Golden-crowned Kinglet

Regulus satrapa

LENGTH: 3"–4" (75–102 mm)

WHAT TO LOOK FOR: small size; center of crown orange (male) or yellow (female); greenish above, with white eye stripe and wing bars.

HABITAT: coniferous forests; other forests, thickets (migration, winter).

CHARACTERISTICS: Restless, flitting movements and a very small size are good signs that the bird you are looking at is a kinglet. Scarcely pausing to perch, kinglets glean small insects and their eggs from leaves and bark. In its fluttering flight the golden-crowned kinglet utters a high, thin *sssst*, which is often repeated several times as a phrase.

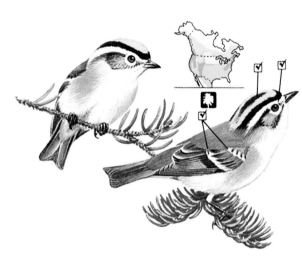

Ruby-crowned Kinglet

Regulus calendula

LENGTH: 3 1/2"–4" (89–102 mm)

WHAT TO LOOK FOR: small size; greenish above, with white eye ring and wing bars; red crown (male); often flicks wings.

HABITAT: coniferous forests; other woodlands, thickets (migration, winter).

CHARACTERISTICS: The ruby crown of this kinglet is worn only by the males, and even on them it is not always evident. (The amount of red that shows seems to depend on how agitated the kinglet is.) Though a mere mite of a bird, it has a loud and varied song, and ornithologists from Audubon on have mentioned how astonished they were the first time they heard a ruby-crowned kinglet sing.

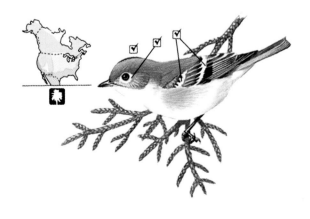

Blue-gray Gnatcatcher *Polioptila caerulea*

LENGTH: 4"–5" (10–13 cm)

WHAT TO LOOK FOR: slim, long-tailed bird; blue-gray above, white below; tail blackish, with white outer feathers; white eye ring.

HABITAT: mixed and oak forests, chaparral, open pinyon-juniper forests, thickets and groves along rivers.

CHARACTERISTICS: This tiny bird darts from perch to perch, uttering its thin, mewing *spee,* flicking its long tail, and feeding on minute insects. In the breeding season the male has a soft, warbling song. He assists with the building of the nest, which may be located as low as 3 feet (90 cm) or as high as 80 feet (24.6 m) above the ground. The structure is roughly the shape of an acorn with the top hollowed out, and it consists of various fine materials, including plant down, petals, feathers, and hair.

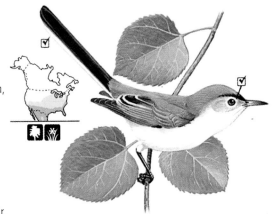

Warbling Vireo *Vireo gilvus*

LENGTH: 4½"–5½" (11–14 cm)

WHAT TO LOOK FOR: no conspicuous markings; grayish green above, white below.

HABITAT: open mixed and deciduous forests; groves; orchards; shade trees in towns and suburbs.

CHARACTERISTICS: Fourteen species of vireos nest in North America. The warbling vireo and a few others have continent-wide ranges. They are noted for the leisurely pace of their activity, compared with that of kinglets and warblers, with which they are often seen on migration. They also have thicker bills.

Red-eyed Vireo

Vireo olivaceus

LENGTH: 5"–6½" (13–17 cm)

WHAT TO LOOK FOR: white eye stripe; gray cap; greenish above, white below; no wing bars.

HABITAT: deciduous woodlands, open areas with scattered trees, suburbs.

CHARACTERISTICS: During the breeding season the male red-eyed vireo is a persistent singer, delivering lengthy passages of short, two- to six-note phrases. The bird tends to go on so long that he used to be nicknamed "preacher." Usually he sings at normal volume, but in courtship he also has a "whisper song," sometimes quite different in character from the regular song.

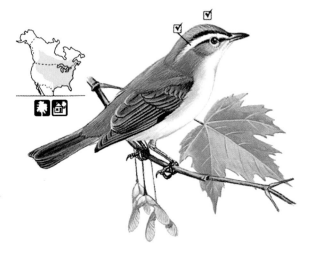

Black-and-white Warbler

Mniotilta varia

LENGTH: 4"–5½" (10–14 cm)

WHAT TO LOOK FOR: streaked black and white above, white below; white stripe through crown; female and immature with white face.

HABITAT: deciduous forests; parks, gardens with trees (migration).

CHARACTERISTICS: Early ornithologists called this species the black-and-white creeper or creeping warbler. Constantly in motion, it searches for insects on bark, moving along head up like a creeper or down like a nuthatch. It has a brisk, sibilant song, usually a string of high-pitched double syllables—*weesee, weesee, weesee, weesee.*

Prothonotary Warbler

Protonotaria citrea

LENGTH: 4½"–5" (11–13 cm)

WHAT TO LOOK FOR: bright orange-yellow head and breast, fading to lighter below; gray wings and tail; female more yellowish.

HABITAT: wooded bottomlands; lowland swamps; moist, frequently flooded woods.

CHARACTERISTICS: Court officers, or prothonotaries in the catholic church, who sometimes wore bright yellow robes, inspired the name of this handsome species. The prothonotary warbler is a bird of wooded swamps and riverbanks. As a rule it nests in a tree cavity or a deserted woodpecker hole, but in some localities it is tame enough to choose a birdhouse or any other small container.

American Redstart

Setophaga ruticilla

LENGTH: 4"–5½" (10–14 cm)

WHAT TO LOOK FOR: male black, with white belly and orangy patches on wings and tail; female and immature grayish above, white below, with yellow patches.

HABITAT: second-growth deciduous forests, thickets, suburbs, parks.

CHARACTERISTICS: One of the most common warblers, this is also one of the most attractive. Flashes of color on the fanned-out wings and tail ("redstart" means "red-tailed") make the lively birds resemble flitting butterflies as they catch insects on the wing. The variable song is a set of single or double notes on one pitch, which may end with a higher or lower note—*zee-zee-zee-zee-zee-zeeo.*

Female

Male

Northern Waterthrush

Seiurus noveboracensis

LENGTH: 5"–6" (13–15 cm)

WHAT TO LOOK FOR: pale eye stripe; dark brown above, buffy with dark streaks below; teeters continually.

HABITAT: wet woodlands; brushy areas (migration).

CHARACTERISTICS: Look and listen for this warbler near placid water. The closely related Louisiana waterthrush (*Seiurus motacilla*) is more likely near fast-flowing streams. Both species bob and teeter along over banks, rocks, and logs. Their looks are similar, but with practice they can be distinguished by their voices. Both build their nests, of moss and other bits of vegetation, near water.

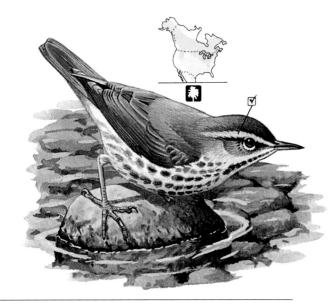

Ovenbird *Seiurus aurocapilla*

LENGTH: 5"–6" (13–15 cm)

WHAT TO LOOK FOR: olive above, with orange crown bordered by black; white below, with dark streaks; white eye ring; pinkish legs; walks on ground.

HABITAT: deciduous woodlands.

CHARACTERISTICS: Once it has become familiar, the voice of the ovenbird is one of the most obvious in the woods. The song begins softly and builds to a ringing crescendo— *teacher, teacher, teacher, teacher!* The ovenbird is a ground-dwelling warbler. Its covered nest, which accounts for its name, is generally hidden on the forest floor.

Common Yellowthroat

Geothlypis trichas

LENGTH: 4"–5½" (10–14 cm)

WHAT TO LOOK FOR: male with black mask, edged above with white; greenish brown above, with yellow throat, upper breast, and undertail; female without mask.

HABITAT: wet brushy areas, freshwater and saltwater marshes.

CHARACTERISTICS: This familiar warbler, black-masked like a little bandit, is usually first seen peering at the intruder from the depths of a shrub or thicket. Sooner or later, the yellowthroat announces itself with a rhythmic *witchery, witchery, witchery* or variations on that theme. Yellowthroats sometimes nest in loose colonies, but most often breeding pairs are well distributed through brushy or marshy areas.

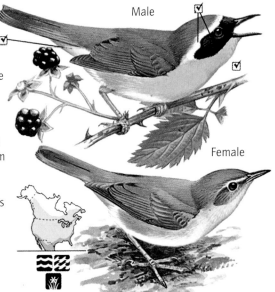

Male

Female

Yellow-breasted Chat

Icteria virens

LENGTH: 6½"–7½" (17–19 cm)

WHAT TO LOOK FOR: largest warbler; dark mask; heavy bill; white "spectacles", green above; yellow breast.

HABITAT: dense thickets and tangles, usually near water; shrubby areas in upland pastures.

CHARACTERISTICS: For years ornithologists have been saying that this bird is in all probability not really a warbler. It is half again as big as some species, and much more robust. Its song is loud and varied. One observer who tried to put a passage into syllables got this result "*C-r-r-r-r-r–whirr–that's it–chee–quack, cluck–yit-yit-yit–now hit it–tr-r-r–when–caw, caw–cut, cut–tea-boy–who, who–mew, mew*–and so on till you are tired of listening."

Palm Warbler

Dendroica palmarum

LENGTH: 4"–5½" (10–14 cm)

WHAT TO LOOK FOR: reddish cap (breeding); underparts yellow or whitish, streaked, with yellow undertail; wags tail.

HABITAT: forest swamps, bogs; brushy areas (migration, winter).

CHARACTERISTICS: Ornithologists first observed this warbler wintering among the palms of Florida, hence its common name—surely a misnomer for a species breeding in northern bogs. During migration the palm warbler is often seen on the ground or in a low tree, where it flicks its tail up and down.

Yellow-rumped Warbler

Dendroica coronata

LENGTH: 41/2"–51/2" (11–14 cm)

what to look for: male with yellow crown, rump, and shoulder patch, white (East) or yellow (West) throat, black bib, white tail patches (visible mainly in flight); female and immature paler, browner.

HABITAT: coniferous and mixed forests; other woodlands, thickets (migration, winter).

CHARACTERISTICS: This is one of the most abundant of our warblers, and at times in migration it seems to outnumber all the others combined. It has a bright, loud chip call that is easily learned, but recognizing its trilling song takes practice. Audubon's warbler (the western subspecies) and the eastern myrtle were long considered separate species.

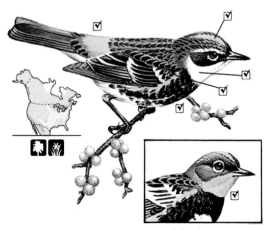

Audubon's Warbler

Yellow Warbler
Dendroica petechia

LENGTH: 4"–5" (10–13 cm)

WHAT TO LOOK FOR: mostly yellow (more greenish above); male streaked with reddish on breast; female duller.

HABITAT: riverside woodlands, wet thickets, brushy marsh edges, orchards, suburbs, parks.

CHARACTERISTICS: This species has the largest breeding range of any warbler and is common not only in most of North America but as far south as Peru. The yellow warbler often nests in willows, alders, or other shrubs along the edge of a swamp or road; its neat cup of silvery plant fibers is usually built in a low fork.

The male is a persistent singer with two basic songs: *pip-pip-pip-sissewa-is sweet* and *wee-see-wee-see-wiss-wiss-u.*

Female

Male

Bobolink
Dolichonyx oryzivorus

LENGTH: 5½"–7½" (14–19 cm)

WHAT TO LOOK FOR: breeding male black, with back of head yellowish and much white on wings and lower back; other plumages buffy, heavily streaked above.

HABITAT: moist open fields, meadows, farmlands, marshes (migration).

CHARACTERISTICS: The jumbled tinkling of the bobolink's song seems to come from every quarter of the wet meadow or grainfield where the bird nests. The male may be sitting on a weed stalk or fence post or in a tree along the edge; he may be hovering on beating wings or dashing after a female in courtship. Once the breeding season is over, the singing ceases. The male molts into a plumage like that of his mate, and flocks of bobolinks fly to South America, calling *pink* from time to time as they go.

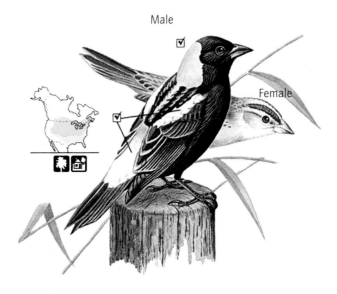

Male

Female

Western Meadowlark
Sturnella neglecta

LENGTH: 8"–10½" (20–27 cm)

WHAT TO LOOK FOR: black V across bright yellow underparts; outer tail feathers white; streaked brown above.

HABITAT: prairies, meadows, open areas.

CHARACTERISTICS: Lewis and Clark first noticed the differences between this species and the Eastern meadowlark (*Sturnella magna*), which look much alike but differ greatly in song. When Audubon rediscovered the Western meadowlark in 1843, the scientific name he gave it poked fun at the long time between sightings: it means "neglected meadowlark." Many who have heard the songs of both meadowlarks believe that the sweet, melancholy phrases of the eastern bird cannot compare with the rich, flutelike bubbling of the western.

Western   Eastern

Red-winged Blackbird
Agelaius phoeniceus

LENGTH: 7"–9½" (18–24 cm)

WHAT TO LOOK FOR: male black, with yellow-bordered red shoulder patch; female dark brown, heavily streaked; immature male like female but with red patch.

HABITAT: swamps, marshes, adjacent open areas, farmlands.

CHARACTERISTICS: The male red-winged blackbird's song is a herald of spring. *Con-ka-ree*, he calls, as if proclaiming victory over winter. Red-wings feed and roost in flocks, but in late summer the flocks vanish. They have retired to some marsh, where the birds hide in the vegetation, molt their flight feathers, and grow new ones. Then the flocks reappear, headed south.

Male

Female

Brown-headed Cowbird

Molothrus ater

LENGTH: 6"–8" (15–20 cm)

WHAT TO LOOK FOR: conical bill; male glossy black, with dark brown head; female gray, with paler throat.

HABITAT: farmlands, groves, forest edges, river woodlands.

CHARACTERISTICS: Few birds are as generally disapproved of as the brown-headed cowbird, which lays its eggs in the nests of other birds, particularly flycatchers, sparrows, vireos, and warblers. A newly hatched cowbird quickly grows larger than the rightful nestlings and devours most of the food; it may even push the hosts' young out of the nest. The foster parents feed the huge intruder until it can fly.

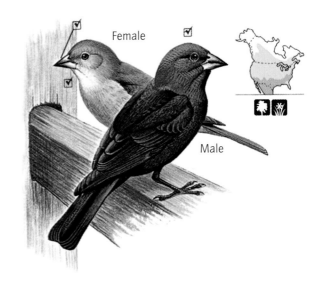

Female

Male

Yellow-headed Blackbird

Xanthocephalus xanthocephalus

LENGTH: 8"–10" (20–25 cm)

what to look for: male black, with yellow head and breast and white wing patches; female brown, with dull yellow on face and breast and white throat.

HABITAT: freshwater marshes, adjacent open areas.

CHARACTERISTICS: This handsome species nests over water 24–48 inches (60–120 cm) deep, and may abandon a nest if the water level drops. The nests are slung between reed stems and are woven of soggy blades of dead grass.

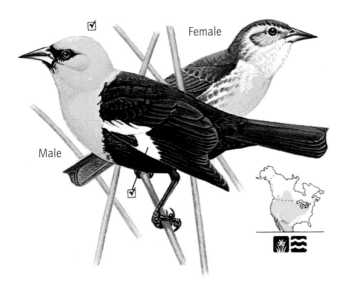

Female

Male

Common Grackle *Quiscalus quiscula*

LENGTH: 10"–12½" (25–32 cm)

WHAT TO LOOK FOR: long keel-shaped tail; long pointed bill; light yellow eye; male glossy black, with purple, bronze, or greenish cast; female less glossy.

HABITAT: farmlands, groves, suburbs, parks.

CHARACTERISTICS: Before the trees have begun to leaf out in the North, the common grackles arrive. Soon courting males are posturing in the treetops, puffing up their glossy plumage, spreading their long tails, and uttering their rasping *chu-seeck*. Larger species of grackles are the great-tailed (*Quiscalus mexicanus*) of southwestern farmlands and the boat-tailed (*Quiscalus major*), a salt-marsh bird.

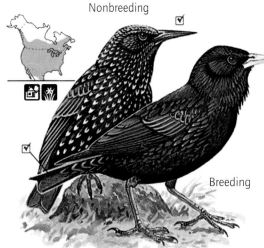

Nonbreeding

Breeding

European Starling *Sturnus vulgaris*

LENGTH: 7"–8½" (18–22 cm)

WHAT TO LOOK FOR: long pointed bill; short, square tail; black overall, with greenish and purple gloss (nonbreeding with light spots); immature brownish, darker above.

HABITAT: farmlands, open woodlands, brushy areas, towns, cities.

CHARACTERISTICS: In 1890 the efforts to introduce this European bird to North America succeeded, and descendants of the 100 birds released in New York City began to spread across the land. The starling's habit of gathering in huge roosts has made it a pest in many areas, and it deprives many hole-nesting species of their homes. It does, however, eat many destructive insects.

Brewer's Blackbird

Euphagus cyanocephalus

LENGTH: 7½"–9½" (19–24 cm)

WHAT TO LOOK FOR: male black, with yellow eye and purple gloss on head; female grayish brown, darker above, with dark eye; tail proportionately shorter than grackle's.

HABITAT: open areas.

CHARACTERISTICS: Two medium-sized blackbirds closely resemble one another—this species and the rusty blackbird (*Euphagus carolinus*). In winter they may be found in many of the same regions, but Brewer's blackbird frequents grassy areas and the rusty blackbird swampy woods. Brewer's gives a strong rough whistle or a "whirring gurgle", the rusty calls *tickle-EE*, sounding like a mechanical joint that needs oiling.

Female

Male

Baltimore/Bullock's Oriole

Icterus galbula/Icterus bullockii

LENGTH: 6"–7½" (15–19 cm)

WHAT TO LOOK FOR: pointed bill; male orange, with black on head, throat, back, wings, and tail; female and immature pale yellow or orange below, brownish above, with white wing bars.

HABITAT: open deciduous woodlands; shade trees in farmlands, towns, cities.

CHARACTERISTICS: A liquid, whistled song and a flash of color at the top of a tall tree signal the presence of an oriole. Scientists have recently returned these orioles to two species, having merged them in the 1950s. Where the eastern Baltimore and western Bullock's ranges overlap in mid-continent there is some interbreeding, but not enough to consider them a valid species. The Baltimore's nest is the familiar deep pouch swinging at the end of a slender limb; its western cousin's is often tied to twigs at the top and sides.

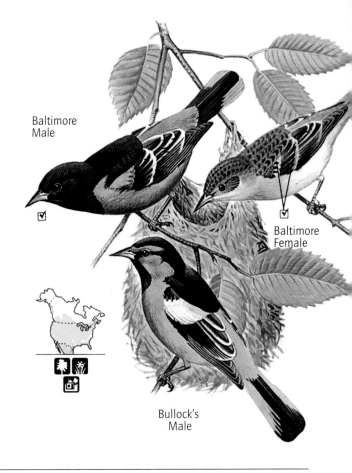

Baltimore Male

Baltimore Female

Bullock's Male

Female

Male

Summer Tanager

Piranga rubra

LENGTH: 6"–7½" (15–19 cm)

WHAT TO LOOK FOR: yellowish bill; male red; female yellowish green above, yellow below.

HABITAT: woodlands; in uplands, drier forests of oak, hickory, or pine.

CHARACTERISTICS: Tanagers are mainly insect eaters, though they do take some buds and fruit. The summer tanager is especially fond of beetles and bees, and it will tear wasps' nests apart to get at the larvae. The hard parts of beetles are not digested, but are coughed up as pellets. This species builds a flimsy nest on a horizontal bough. Its song is like a spluttery call is traditionally written as *chicky-tucky-tuck.*

Northern Cardinal

Cardinalis cardinalis

LENGTH: 7"–8½" (18–22 cm)

WHAT TO LOOK FOR: prominent crest; conical reddish bill; male bright red, with black around eye and bill; female brownish yellow, with red on wings and tail.

HABITAT: open woods, forest edges, thickets, suburbs, parks.

CHARACTERISTICS: The cardinal's rich coloring and its readiness to come to feeders have made it a favorite among bird-watchers. Its musical repertoire consists of loud, clear whistles that are usually repeated several times—*wheet, wheet, wheet, wheet, chew, chew, chew, cheedle, cheedle, cheedle*. Male and female may sing alternately, as if in response to each other. Cardinals also have a metallic *pink* note. This species is one of a number of southern birds that have extended their ranges northward during this century. Among the others are the northern mockingbird, tufted titmouse, turkey vulture, and red-bellied woodpecker.

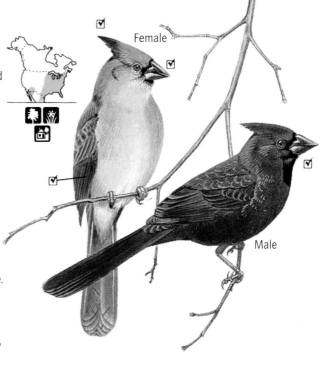

Female

Male

Male

Female

Blue Grosbeak

Posserina caerulea

LENGTH: 6"–7" (15–18 cm)

WHAT TO LOOK FOR: large conical bill; rusty or buffy wing bars; male blue; female brownish, with dark wings.

HABITAT: brushy areas, open woodlands, forests near rivers.

CHARACTERISTICS: Snakeskins are occasionally woven into the nest of the blue grosbeak, sometimes covering the entire outside; other nesting materials include dry leaves, cornhusks, and strips of plastic or newspaper. The female incubates the four eggs for 11 days; the young—fed by both parents, mostly on insects and snails—leave the nest less than two weeks after hatching. For adults, fruit, seed, and other vegetable matter make up perhaps a third of the diet.

Evening Grosbeak

Coccothraustes vespertinus

LENGTH: 7"–8" (18–20 cm)

WHAT TO LOOK FOR: bill large, light-colored, conical; male yellow-brown, with black tail and black and white wings; female paler, grayish.

HABITAT: coniferous forests; other forests and at feeders (migration, winter).

CHARACTERISTICS: The evening grosbeak was given its name by an observer who heard a flock at twilight, at a site northwest of Lake Superior. At that time— 1823—the evening grosbeak was a western species; since then, it has spread far to the east. One hypothesis is that feeding trays loaded with sunflower seed may have played a part in this expansion, but reports show that grosbeaks regularly pass up such offerings in favor of boxelder seed and other wild food.

Female

Indigo Bunting

Passerina cyanea

LENGTH: 4½"–5½" (11–14 cm)

WHAT TO LOOK FOR: male indigo-blue, with blackish wings and tail, no wing bars; female brown above, whitish below, with faint streaking on breast.

HABITAT: brushy areas, scrubby fields, forest edges.

CHARACTERISTICS: The male indigo bunting is one of the few birds giving full-voiced performances at midday. A typical song has been written down as *sir, chewe, chewe, cheer, cheer, swe, swe, chir, chir chir, sir, sir, see, see, fish, fish, fish*. The western lazuli bunting (*Passerina amoena*), with sky blue head, rusty breast, and wing bars, interbreeds with the indigo where their ranges overlap.

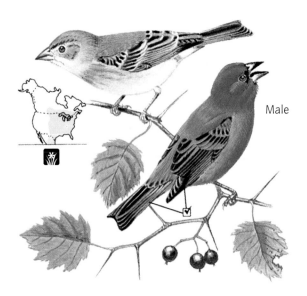

Male

Black-headed Grosbeak
Pheucticus melanocephalus

LENGTH: 6½"–7½" (17–19 cm)

what to look for: heavy whitish bill; male orangish yellow, with black head and black and white wings; female brownish, with facial pattern and streaks.

HABITAT: open mixed or deciduous woodlands, forest edges, chaparral, orchards, parks.

CHARACTERISTICS: This species is the western counterpart of the rose-breasted grosbeak, and their clear, whistled songs are similar. The usual song of the black-headed grosbeak lasts about five seconds, but may be longer; a male once performed for seven hours.

Male

Female

Painted Bunting *Passerina ciris*

LENGTH: 5"–5½" (13–14 cm)

WHAT TO LOOK FOR: male with blue head, red underparts and rump, and green back; female green above, yellowish below.

HABITAT: brushy fields, forest edges, shrubby streamsides, fencerows, towns.

CHARACTERISTICS: Considered by many to be North America's most beautifully colored bird, the male painted bunting justly merits the nickname "nonpareil" (unequaled). Males are very conspicuous as they sing from high, exposed perches, but the species favors thick ground cover and shrubbery for feeding and nesting. The majority of painted buntings migrate to Central America, though some may overwinter in Florida.

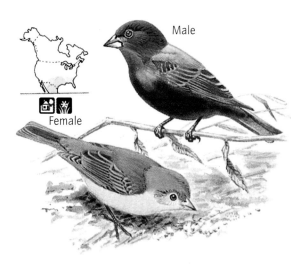

Male

Female

Purple Finch *Carpodacus purpureus*

LENGTH: 5¼"–6" (13–15 cm)

WHAT TO LOOK FOR: male with white belly and raspberry red head, upperparts, and breast; female brown above, heavily streaked below, with broad white stripe behind eye.

HABITAT: mixed woodlands, suburbs, and at feeders (migration, winter).

CHARACTERISTICS: These handsome finches move erratically from place to place, often in large numbers. In winter an area with few or no purple finches one day may have thousands the next. Flocks may consist mostly or solely of brightly colored males or of brown females and immatures. In late summer purple finches begin to molt, and in winter plumage the males' reddish areas appear frosted. With wear, the whitish tinge disappears, revealing the rich breeding color.

Female

Male

Red Crossbill *Loxia curvirostra*

LENGTH: 5½"–6" (14–15 cm)

WHAT TO LOOK FOR: crossed tips of bill; male brick red, with dark wings and tail; female greenish yellow, lighter below.

HABITAT: coniferous forests; occasionally in other woodlands.

CHARACTERISTICS: The two crossbills—the red and the white-winged (*Loxia leucoptera*)—are nomads, following the seed crops of conifers or sometimes other forest trees. Their choice of when to nest also seems to depend on the cone supply; they will nest in early spring or even late winter if food is plentiful. A crossbill uses its beak to pry apart the scales of a cone while the tongue extracts the seed.

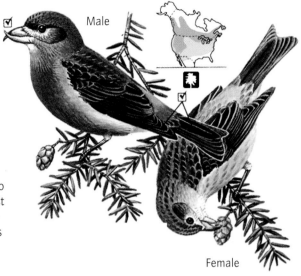

Male

Female

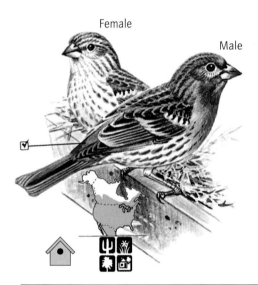

Female

Male

House Finch *Carpodacus mexicanus*

LENGTH: 5"–5½" (13–14 cm)

WHAT TO LOOK FOR: male with bright red head, breast, and rump; female dull brown, with faintly streaked breast and no eye stripe.

HABITAT: deserts, scrubby areas, open forests, farmlands, towns, suburbs; at feeders.

CHARACTERISTICS: The house finch is an exceptionally adaptable species. Once restricted to the Southwest, it began to extend its range in the 1920s; following the release of caged birds in New York in 1940, house finches spread in the East. The birds nest in all sorts of sites—in holes in trees, among cactus spines, on the beams of buildings, and in the nests of other birds. In the West, Cassin's finch (*Carpodacus cassinii*) may be mistaken for this species or for the purple finch.

Eastern/Spotted Towhee

Pipilo erythrophthalmus/Pipilo maculatus

LENGTH: 7"–8" (18–20 cm)

what to look for: male mostly black and white, with rufous flanks and white on wings and tail; white spots on back (spotted towee); female with brown instead of black.

HABITAT: thickets, open forests, brushy fields, chaparral, suburbs, parks.

CHARACTERISTICS: A loud, buzzy shree or shrank from the underbrush and vigorous scratching in the leaves announce the presence of an Eastern towhee. Its song is often transcribed as drink–your-teeeee. In the West, the spotted towhee sounds much like its eastern cousin. They are common in suburban yards.

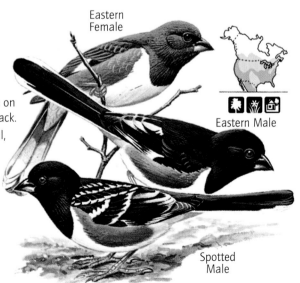

Eastern Female

Eastern Male

Spotted Male

Savannah Sparrow *Passerculus sandwichensis*

LENGTH: 4"–6" (10–15 cm)

WHAT TO LOOK FOR: streaked above, heavily streaked below; light yellowish stripe above eye; short tail; varies from pale to dark.

HABITAT: tundra, prairies, meadows, salt marshes, beaches.

CHARACTERISTICS: When alarmed, the Savannah sparrow seems to prefer running through the grass to flying. When it does fly up it usually skims over the grass very briefly, then drops out of sight. Males often sing from a weed-top perch. The song—*tsip-tsip-tsip-seeeee-saaaaay*—ends in a two-part trill that at a distance is all that can be heard. "Savannah" is a fair description of the bird's habitat, but the name actually refers to the Georgia city where the first specimen was found.

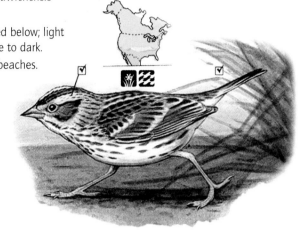

Dark-eyed Junco *Junco hyemalis*

LENGTH: 5"–6½" (13–17 cm)

WHAT TO LOOK FOR: white outer tail feathers; light pink bill; white belly; rest of plumage slate gray (with or without white wing bars) or rusty brown with dark head and pinkish brown flanks.

HABITAT: coniferous and mixed forests; forest edges and at feeders (winter).

CHARACTERISTICS: Until recently, the birds shown here were considered separate species. A third form was the white-winged junco, found in a limited range in the West. All three are now believed to be races of a single species, and have been lumped under the name dark-eyed junco. A fourth form, the gray-headed, common in the Southwest, was recently added to this species.

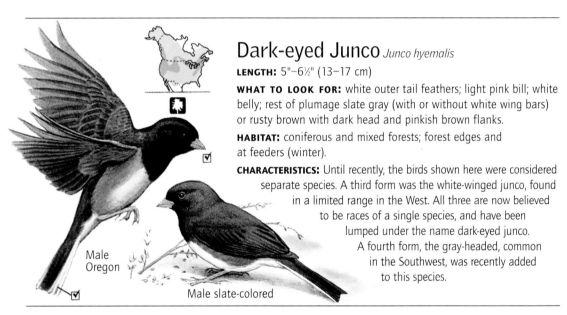

Male Oregon

Male slate-colored

American Tree Sparrow

Spizella arborea

LENGTH: 5½"–6½" (14–17 cm)

WHAT TO LOOK FOR: reddish cap and eye streak; dark spot in center of pale gray breast.

HABITAT: sub-arctic areas with stunted trees; brushy areas, grasslands, woodland edges, weedy fields, and at feeders (winter).

CHARACTERISTICS: Preferring underbrush and shrubs to trees, American tree sparrows nest on the ground in dense thickets in the Far North. Whether they appear in large numbers in more southerly regions during winter months depends on the severity of the weather. When the warmth of spring returns, the birds' tinkling song can be heard before they depart for their northern nesting grounds.

Chipping Sparrow

Spizella passerina

LENGTH: 4½"–5½" (11–14 cm)

WHAT TO LOOK FOR: reddish cap; white stripe above eye; black eye streak; pale grayish below; immature with streaky brown cap.

HABITAT: open woodlands, forest edges, farmlands, orchards, suburbs, parks.

CHARACTERISTICS: The "chippy" is named for its song—a trill or string of musical chips, varying from quite long to very brief. It normally sings from a perch in a tree, often an evergreen. Evergreens are also favorite nesting sites, although the birds may be found raising young in orchard trees, in dooryard vines and shrubbery, and occasionally even on the ground.

Immature

Male

Female

House Sparrow (English Sparrow)

Passer domesticus

LENGTH: 5"–6" (13–15 cm)

WHAT TO LOOK FOR: male with black, whitish, gray, and reddish on head and breast; female brownish above, grayer below.

HABITAT: farms, suburbs, cities.

CHARACTERISTICS: Most people regret the efforts made in the 19th century to transplant the house sparrow from Europe. House sparrows, which belong to a completely different family from our native sparrows, drive bluebirds, wrens, and other songbirds from nesting sites; they tear up nests, destroy eggs, and toss out nestlings. The species reached its peak early in this century. Since then, numbers have declined, probably because of the scarcity of horses and therefore of the waste horse feed eaten by the birds.

Field Sparrow *Spizella pusilla*

LENGTH: 5"–6" (13–15 cm)

WHAT TO LOOK FOR: pinkish bill, reddish cap; buffy below; immature with streaked cap and buffy chest band.

HABITAT: fields, meadows, forest edges.

CHARACTERISTICS: The sweet song of the field sparrow is a series of whistled notes delivered slowly at first and then accelerated into a rapid run. In spring, males establish territories by singing and by chasing their neighbors; once a male is mated, he sings far less than before. Early in the season, nest sites are on the ground or only a short distance above it. As the season advances and the pairs begin second and third families, fewer ground nests are attempted. Nests, however, are seldom more than 3 feet (90 cm) above the ground.

Immature

White-crowned Sparrow
Zonotrichia leucophrys

LENGTH: 5½"–7" (14–18 cm)

WHAT TO LOOK FOR: crown broadly striped with black and white (light and dark brown on immature); gray breast; pink or yellowish bill; pale throat.

HABITAT: mountain thickets, areas with scattered brush and trees; roadsides, suburbs (winter).

CHARACTERISTICS: The trim, elegant white-crowned sparrow breeds in brushy, open terrain, whether in the subarctic, in western mountains, or along the Pacific Coast. The nest site is usually on or near the ground. Male and female approach the nest differently: the male flies in directly; the female lands 10–15 feet (3–4.6 m) away, then moves in by stages, pausing often to perch.

Immature

Immature

White-throated Sparrow
Zonotrichia albicollis

LENGTH: 5½"–6½" (14–17 cm)

WHAT TO LOOK FOR: white throat; gray breast; black and white striped crown, often with yellow patch in front of eye (crown of immature with brown and buff stripes).

HABITAT: woodlands with dense brush; brushy areas, forest edges (migration, winter).

CHARACTERISTICS: The white-throat is often nicknamed the Canada bird or the Peabody bird, in imitation of a typical song, written as "Oh, sweet Canada, Canada, Canada," or "Poor Sam Peabody, Peabody, Peabody." The white-throat is abundant and whistles its sweet song loudly and not too fast.

Snow Bunting *Plectrophenax nivalis*

LENGTH: 5½"–7" (14–18 cm)

WHAT TO LOOK FOR: mostly white; breeding male with black on back, wings, and tail; non-breeding male with reddish brown on head and shoulders; female paler.

HABITAT: tundra; prairies, meadows, beaches (migration, winter).

CHARACTERISTICS: The snowflakes or snow birds breed farther north than any other species of songbird. The males arrive on their arctic breeding grounds by mid-May, three or four weeks earlier than the females. The Eskimos welcome them as harbingers of spring. Snow buntings nest mainly on rocky terrain, usually building their bulky fur- and feather-lined nests in holes and crannies. In winter they flock along coasts and in open country; they feed on fallen grain in fields and pastures and on weed seed, as well as on sand fleas and other insects.

Ruby-throated Hummingbird

Archilochus colubris

LENGTH: 3"–3½" (75–89 mm)

WHAT TO LOOK FOR: bill long, needlelike; metallic green above; throat metallic red (male) or dingy white (female).

HABITAT: deciduous and mixed forests; rural, suburban, and city gardens.

CHARACTERISTICS: Of the 13 species of hummingbird that regularly nest north of Mexico, this is the only one breeding east of the Great Plains. The broad-tailed hummingbird (*Selasphorus platycercus*) of western mountains is similar in appearance, but the ranges of the two do not overlap. "Hummers," unlike other birds, can fly backwards or straight up and down. They can also hover, and are able to drink flower nectar without actually landing on the blossom. The flowers they drink from are usually long, tubular, and orange or red.

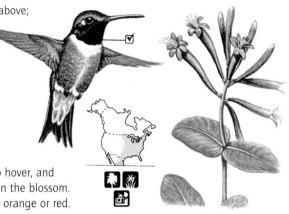

Rufous Hummingbird

Selasphorus rufus

LENGTH: 3½"–4" (89–102 mm)

WHAT TO LOOK FOR: male mostly red-brown, with iridescent orange-red throat and sides of head; female with green back, rufous on flanks and base of tail feathers.

HABITAT: alpine meadows, edges of woodlands; lowlands (migration).

CHARACTERISTICS: The rufous hummingbird flies farther north than any other hummingbird. As the birds move south toward Mexico (mainly in July and August) they may be found as high in the mountains as 13,200 feet (4,061 m). Hummingbirds are generally feisty, but this species is particularly pugnacious. Yet at times rufous hummingbirds appear to breed in colonies, with some females nesting only a few feet from one another.

Black-chinned Hummingbird

Archilochus alexandri

LENGTH: 3"–3¾" (75–95 mm)

WHAT TO LOOK FOR: back metallic green; throat black, bordered with iridescent purple (male); slightly forked tail.

HABITAT: dry scrub, woodlands near streams, wooded canyons, mountain meadows, gardens.

CHARACTERISTICS: Hummingbirds are unique to the New World. European explorers were astounded by the tiny glittering creatures that zipped up and down, and backwards, with wings humming and blurred. Hummingbirds perform set figures in courtship flights. The male black-chinned hummingbird, for instance, swings in pendulum-like arcs above the female; at the top of each swoop he comes to a dead stop.

Index